THIS JOURNAL BELONGS TO:

Connie Opfell

Designer: Katie Benezra

ISBN: 978-1-4197-2884-6

© 2017 Abrams Noterie

Printed and bound in the United States

10 9 8 7 6 5 4 3 2 1

Abrams Noterie products are available at special discounts when
purchased in quantity for premiums and promotions as well as fundraising
or educational use. Special editions can also be created to specification.
For details, contact specialsales@abramsbooks.com or the address below.

ABRAMS
The Art of Books

115 West 18th Street
New York, NY 10011
abramsbooks.com

4/14/2017

In the first 100 days of the Trump presidency, so an "Alternative Facts" journal seems like a good idea - both to enjoy a laugh at this ridiculous and very scary time, and to push myself to reflect. I haven't been taking time to reflect much over the past year or so - it's time.

What I have been doing is shifting between obsessively watching/reading about the news and avoiding by playing games. And though I do feel present while going through life tasks I mostly feel like I'm in a dream state, pushed to act through necessity only, and otherwise living in inertia.

Jan spoke of her depression recently, and acted as though we shared that - I was surprised by that. Don't feel depressed - vacillate between feeling happy and feeling a bit anxious, mostly because I have so little patience to act -

Haven't been doing yoga or meditating – They have left my routine, in favor of games and news. I'm not pleased about that. I also have a slew of unstarted projects that lie on the periphery of my life + actually some started but left to stagnate. While I alliviate my anxiety with routine and games.

No clue what the source of anxiety really is. So many options – aging, impending death of my parents, feeling alone, knowing that I won't live long enough to see "what happens" – that's my death fear – that I won't be around for the next thing, whatever it is, missing out.

So maybe that's the big issue that underlies my inertia – the fear of death. I think of myself as ok with dying, of not afraid of being gone – even of pain – but I do want to be around to know my neices & nephews' families, and to see what happens in my family's & friends' lives.

6/28/19 - Home from a week-long stay with Dylan, spent driving her to Princeton House day treatment (DBT pgm) ~~as~~ during the week & to Home Depot (her job) last weekend. Started with a move-out of her stuff from Bree's apartment.

I feel very touched by the experience with her. She's feeling particularly vulnerable, and yet there's a strength that is seeing her through this time and helping her use humor and music to help Bree through it too.

She (he) "came out" to the group yesterday. Talked about the support she recieved from the group — or rather, from a couple of the guys that had ~~it~~ known. She also talked about her feelings about people's lapses in the he/she thing—

and acknowledges that she sometimes [sic]
also forgets to call himself a he.

She told me her diagnoses —
Major Depression & BPD — and her
medications, and that she thinks the
Dx's fit. She & Bree discuss all
this openly — and despite their
very frequent communication
they clearly miss the together
part of their relationship.

We went to the beach a couple
of times. She did homework. We
talked about a lot of things.

I was straight with her about —
- Bree can't be a good mom, and
she can't be a good dad, if
either of them is unstable.
- Both she and Bree need lots of
time to get their acts together.
- Both of them need to focus on
growing up — creating
an adult life.
- common that people in LGBT
community struggle w/ MI &

alcohol / drug dependency – I think
a lot because of how culture deals
with them.

She is all about me being
wonderful, sadly. Dooms me to
fail in her eyes.

I got her to Buddha & the
Borderline to read. Told her to
get air in her bike's tires.

I noticed:
– She got very ramped up at
the phoniness of the candidates
in the debate.
– She is not very attuned to the
cats' needs – OK, but could be
lots better.
– She acknowledged feeling suicidal
on the day I thought she seemed
to be doing v. well, said she
made a conscious choice not to.
– She is using a lot of the skills
she is learning at P.H.

- She is fairly unstable, but better. Glad she is doing what she's doing.
- She is uncomfortable about AA, more comfortable w/ NA, but still doesn't want to go w/out sponsor.
- She's working on being more honest — clearly has a history of saying what she thinks people want to hear.
- She feels very ecstatic w/ Bree, and also v. insecure/jealous.
- Uses denial a lot — said she keeps telling herself Bree will be there when she ~~gets~~ wakes up & being disappointed.

I think she should probably move to a house w/ other Recovering addicts — would give good support — once she gets her car back & graduates.

3/20/2020 - Day 10 of my
self-enforced quarantine.
Saw this today & want
to adapt/adopt it.

Daily Quarantine Questions
1 - What am I GRATEFUL for
today?
2 - Who am I Checking In With
or CONNECTING WITH Today?
3 - What Expectations of "normal"
am I letting GO OF today?
4 - How am I getting outside
today?
5 - How am I Moving My
Body today?
6 - What BEAUTY am I
either creating, cultivating,
or inviting in today?

10/8/2023

My birthday (72nd) is tomorrow — actually, in about an hour. Feels like it's time to take stock. And I'm stoned for the first time in a few months, so I have a little energy.

For a long time — really since I got cancer 12 years ago — I have been focused on my body falling apart. Feeding it a vegetarian diet and constantly changing supplements, medication & foods to try to make the nausea go away, giving it exercise and stretching to try to resurrect flexibility and ease. Changing my outlook and emotional behavior to lower stress. And spending way too much time listening to the news and playing video games, which I suppose is at least in part both part of the same thing and a distraction from it.

At the same time, I'm making progress on a few goals: Getting ready to move, hopefully, to Foulkeways. Becoming a bridge teacher, as I move through the Intermediate level of players. And I've lost another 15 lbs or so this year in my continued effort to stress my hips and knees less. And I'm feeling more aligned in my relationships with friends. By aligned, I think I mean more reciprocity than before — way less drama and emotion — mostly because I've let some people loose.

I'm ok with being 72. It is what it is. Life is mostly good.

TWO DAYS INTO THE TRUMP PRESIDENCY,
the thesaurus gained a new synonym for falsehoods,
lies, distortion, deception, and total BS (take your pick).
The phrase "alternative facts" has sparked laughter
at its absurdity, but also disbelief and fear that this
administration shows no hesitation in blatantly rewriting
the truth to fit its narrative.

In response, this journal offers an opportunity to ground
yourself in reality, to collect and record in writing
whatever you wish, and to check your own alternative
facts. Use it to make your to-do list or your won't-do list.
Jot down your thoughts, note your lack of ideas, keep
track of your dreams, and collect your nightmares.

Here is one fact: A portion of proceeds from the sale of
this journal will support freedom of the press.